BIBLE 1207
DANIEL

Author:	**Barry G. Burrus, M.Div, M.A., B.S.**
Editor:	Alan Christopherson, M.S.
Illustrations:	John W. Mitchell
	Kyle R. Bennett, A.S.

Alpha Omega Publications ®

300 North McKemy Avenue, Chandler, Arizona 85226-2618
© MM by Alpha Omega Publications, Inc. All rights reserved.
LIFEPAC is a registered trademark of Alpha Omega Publications, Inc.

DANIEL

The book of Daniel, written in both Hebrew and Aramaic, is one of the most studied books of the Old Testament. In the Christian Bible, it is one of the Prophets, while for the Jews, it is included among the Writings. Hebrew canonical scholars claim that while Daniel possessed the prophetic gift, he did not possess the office of prophet. A person who held the office of prophet was one with the prophetic gift who was also raised up and empowered by God to serve as a mediator between the Lord and His people. In Deuteronomy 18:18, God spoke of the coming Prophet, Christ: "I... will put my words in his mouth, and he shall speak unto them all that I shall command him." Daniel's ministry is primarily that of a statesman. He was not only concerned with the people of Judah, but also the kings and kingdoms he had to serve under.

In this LIFEPAC®, you will study Daniel as statesman and prophet, man of conviction and interpreter of dreams. You will then study Daniel's visions and interpretations of them.

OBJECTIVES

Read these objectives. The objectives tell you what you should be able to do when you have successfully completed this LIFEPAC.

When you have finished this LIFEPAC, you should be able to:

1. Describe Daniel's childhood and heritage.
2. Explain Daniel's behavior and convictions while in pagan captivity.
3. Illustrate Daniel's honesty in delivering God's message in every situation.
4. Identify Daniel's concern and intercession for his nation before God.
5. Describe the vision of the four beasts.
6. Describe the vision of the ram and the he-goat.
7. Outline the revelation of the seventy sevens.
8. Describe the vision of the mighty kings.

Survey the LIFEPAC. Ask yourself some questions about this study. Write your questions here.

_____
_____
_____
_____
_____
_____
_____
_____
_____

I. INFLUENCE

Daniel's influence was so great in his lifetime that it penetrated two world empires and effected four mighty monarchs. This humble servant brought God's Word to bear on the Babylonian, Median and Persian empires. He spoke God's truth to their kings: Nebuchadnezzar, Belshazzar, Darius and Cyrus. God effectively used Daniel to minister for His purposes.

SECTION OBJECTIVES

Review these objectives. When you have completed this section, you should be able to:

1. Describe Daniel's childhood and heritage.
2. Explain his behavior and convictions while in pagan captivity.
3. Illustrate his honesty in delivering God's message in all situations.
4. Describe his concern and intercession for his nation before God.

VOCABULARY

Study these words to enhance your learning success in this section.

compatriots	evince	obliterate
debauchery	induce	solicitude
emulation		

Note: All vocabulary words in this LIFEPAC appear in **boldface** print the first time they are used. If you are unsure of the meaning when you are reading, study the definitions given in the Glossary.

 Read Daniel 1, 3, and 1 Corinthians 10:18-33.

CONVICTIONS

From the first mention of Daniel in Scripture, we realize that God destined him to do great things. He was of noble birth and heritage, and in Ezekiel 14:14 and 20, God equates the righteousness of Daniel with that of Noah and Job.

Daniel was a young man of conviction with a noble heritage and a godly purpose, shared with his young Hebrew companions Hananiah, Mishael, and Azariah.

Heritage. From Daniel 1:3 and 6 we learn that Daniel was a royal prince as were Hananiah, Mishael, and Azariah. Comparing these verses to 2 Kings 20:12-21 and Isaiah 39, we conclude that Daniel may have been a descendant from King Hezekiah, one of the last great rulers of Judah prior to the Babylonian Captivity. As a young Hebrew prince, Daniel heard the preaching of the prophets Jeremiah, Habakkuk, and Zephaniah, who ministered during Judah's dark days. As a small boy, Daniel may have observed the reforms of godly King Josiah, who swept the land smashing all idols.

It is likely that these experiences helped mold his character. For the remainder of his life, Daniel unflinchingly followed the Lord, by obeying His laws and regular prayer.

***JOSIAH* DESTROYED HIS KINGDOM'S IDOLS**

Daniel was probably very personable and handsome. Daniel 1:4 states that he had "...no blemish, but (was) well favoured, and skilful in all wisdom, cunning in knowledge, and understanding science, and... *had* ability... to stand in the king's palace..." He and his companions were about fifteen years old when deported to Babylon. Although they had suffered the traumatic experience of being replanted in an alien land, Daniel and his companions were faithful and lived according to their heritage. Their faith in the God of Israel was so strong that they worshipped and praised Him no matter the circumstances.

Their very names are indicative of their godly upbringing and spiritual heritage. The name Daniel means *God is my judge*, and Hananiah means *YHWH shows grace*. The name Azariah means *YHWH helps*, and Mishael means *Who is like God?* The Babylonians (sometimes called the Chaldeans) attempted to eradicate the boys' heritage by changing their names and educating them in the culture of the land. The names of the gods of Babylon were actually incorporated into the names of the Hebrew children; the Chaldeans intended to **obliterate** Jewish culture from their minds and memory. Just as Joseph had his name changed in Egypt (Genesis 41:45), so Daniel's name was changed to *Belteshazzar* (Daniel 1:7), meaning *Bel, protect his life!* (*Bel*, also called *Marduk*, was the chief god of Babylon). Hananiah's name was changed to *Shadrach*, meaning *under the command of Aku* (the Babylonian moon god). Azariah's name was changed to *Abednego*, a name meaning *servant of Nego/Nebo* (or Nabu, the god of learning and writing). Finally, Mishael's name was changed to *Meshach*, probably meaning *who is like Aku?* (the moon god).

The changes in names were intended to **induce** them to adopting the customs of Babylon and destroy their connection to their old nationality. Not only were their names changed, but their new forms of education, language, and diet (Daniel 1:4-5) were intended to impress upon them the permanence of their captivity. For three years, they were bombarded by Babylonian customs and culture. Nevertheless, their faith stood firmly in the midst of paganism and **debauchery**.

✐ **Complete these activities.**

1.1   List the Hebrew names of Daniel and his three friends, their original meanings and the new names given in Babylon.

   a. _____ means _____ changed to _____ .
   b. _____ means _____ changed to _____ .
   c. _____ means _____ changed to _____ .
   d. _____ means _____ changed to _____ .

1.2   What were the six requirements for the young men entering the king's service?

   a. _____
   b. _____
   c. _____
   d. _____
   e. _____
   f. _____

1.3   List the four things used to bombard the Hebrew boys with Babylonian culture.

   a. _____   c. _____
   b. _____   d. _____

✐ **Choose the correct answer.**

1.4   The Lord mentions the righteousness of Daniel with that of Noah and _____ .
   a. Abraham   b. David   c. Job   d. Moses

3

1.5   Daniel may have been a descendant of godly King _____ , who was of the lineage of King David.

         a. Zedekiah   b. Josiah   c. Jeroboam   d. Hezekiah

1.6   As a young boy Daniel probably saw the righteous reforms of King _____ who smashed all idols within his kingdom.

         a. Solomon   b. Josiah   c. Habukkuk   d. Zephaniah

1.7   Two of the most important Babylonian gods were Nebo and _____ .

         a. Mark   b. Venus   c. Marduk   d. Zeus

Under Nebuchadnezzar. Daniel's devotion to God's law was clearly exhibited in his decision not to defile himself with the king's meat and wine. The food was most likely not prepared according to God's Law and likely consisted of unclean animals.

The custom in heathen kingdoms was to sacrifice food and drink to their gods, consecrating their meals by a religious rite. First Corinthians 10 indicates that such sacrifices were made to demons, and in Daniel's day, partaking would have involved self-defilement. Most of the Hebrew youths compromised God's principles and partook of the king's provisions (Daniel 1:10-15), but Daniel and his three friends did not.

Daniel was courteous and gentle in offering an alternative to those in authority over him. He did not outright refuse the food, but humbly requested that he and his companions be permitted to try another course. Ashpenaz did not grant their request because he feared for his own life. So Daniel then pressed his case with the second in command, Melzar, who consented to their plan for a limited ten days. They would eat vegetables and drink water, then if their countenances did not appear fairer and their flesh fatter than that of the other captives, Melzar could do as he pleased. The Lord's intervention on their behalf was **evinced** by their healthiness. Thus, their diet was secured for the full three-year period of their preparation.

When their training was complete, Daniel and his three companions were found to be far superior to the other captives. Nebuchadnezzar declared Daniel and his friends were ten times better than all the magicians and astrologers in Babylon. The moral is: never compromise God's Word, but be gentle and pleasant.

Shortly after Daniel and his friends were elevated to high positions, Nebuchadnezzar honored himself by erecting a colossal statue on the plane of Dura that was ninety feet high and nine feet wide. At the dedication ceremony, all the

DANIEL AND HIS THREE COMPANIONS BEFORE KING NEBUCHADNEZZAR

princes, governors, captains, judges, treasurers, counselors, sheriffs, and rulers of his kingdom were gathered together and instructed to bow down to it; however, Shadrach, Meshach, and Abednego refused. Certain Chaldeans accused Daniel's **compatriots** of insurrection and ingratitude. Nebuchadnezzar's wrath decreed death in a furnace to those who would not comply with his regulation. Considering their youth, captivity in an idolatrous land, and position before the earth's mightiest monarch, their answer was amazing. With no powerful friends to support them and with a promised horrendous death, they stood steadfast and testified of their trust in God. When the king, full of fury, commanded that they be cast into the furnace heated seven times hotter than usual, the

Lord vindicated their faith. The king saw the *bound* Hebrews *walking* in the midst of the fire along with a fourth man who he said looked like the Son of God. In holy fear, Nebuchadnezzar called for them to come forth from the furnace. Not one hair of their heads was singed, their coats were undamaged, and not even the smell of fire was upon them (Daniel 3:28-29). Nebuchadnezzar blessed the true God, the idolatrous ceremony was turned into a holy celebration, and the king decreed that there is no other God that can deliver like the God of Shadrach, Meshach, and Abednego. God's grace led to their promotion to positions of greater authority and power. May their faithful example inspire our faith as well.

Match these items.

1.8	_____	Nebuchadnezzar	a.	prophet who delivered God's word to King Hezekiah
1.9	_____	Melzar	b.	a fellow countryman
1.10	_____	Bel (or Marduk)	c.	the Babylonian monarch
1.11	_____	Ashpenaz	d.	master of Nebuchadnezzar's eunuchs
1.12	_____	Dura	e.	plain in which the image was set up in Babylon
1.13	_____	Chaldeans	f.	leading astray morally
1.14	_____	compatriot	g.	the chief Babylonian god (Daniel renamed for)
1.15	_____	Daniel	h.	subordinate whom Ashpenaz set over Daniel
1.16	_____	debauchery	i.	means *God is my judge*
1.17	_____	Isaiah	j.	another name for Babylonians

Complete these statements.

1.18 Daniel held important positions of influence in the a. _____ , b. _____ , and c. _____ empires.

1.19 Four mighty monarchs to whom Daniel ministered in his lifetime were a. _____ , b. _____ , c. _____ , and d. _____ .

1.20 The book of Daniel is written in both a. _____ and b. _____ , and in the Hebrew Bible it is included among the c. _____ .

1.21 Daniel himself should be regarded primarily as a a. _____ who also had the b. _____ gift.

1.22 Three powerful prophets of God in Judah in Daniel's younger years were a. _____ , b. _____ , and c. _____ .

1.23 When Nebuchadnezzar communed with Daniel and his three companions, he found them a. _____ times better in wisdom and understanding than all the b. _____ and astrologers in his kingdom.

1.24 The colossal statue erected by Nebuchadnezzar was a. _____ feet high and b. _____ feet wide.

1.25 Nebuchadnezzar saw a fourth form walking in the fire, like the _____ .

1.26 When the king saw God's preservation of the three Hebrew young men, he a. _____ the true God, and praised them as His b. _____ .

Complete this activity.

1.27 Why did Shadrach, Meshach, and Abednego stand their ground and trust in God in the face of the threat of death?

_____

_____

_____

_____

_____

_____

_____

_____

 Read Daniel 2, 4, and 5.

INTERPRETER OF DREAMS

Ranking with Solomon, Daniel is considered among the wisest men who ever lived. In Ezekiel 28:3, Daniel's name is used as a standard of wisdom. He is highly regarded with Joseph in his statesmanship and ability to interpret dreams.

His gift. Daniel would be the first to proclaim that all of his abilities were from God. Although God gave gifts of knowledge and skill to all the four Hebrew boys taken into captivity, Daniel received the unique gift of understanding visions and dreams (Daniel 1:17). They were well-versed in the wisdom of Babylon, just as Moses was trained in the wisdom of the Egyptians (Acts 7:22), but God gave them discernment, the ability to separate between truth and falsehood. Because Daniel, like Joseph, lived in a culture where great stress was placed on dream interpretation, Daniel's gift glorified God as the only interpreter. When none of the Chaldeans could communicate the king's dream and its interpretation, Daniel requested that Nebuchadnezzar give him time and then he would bring forth the dream with its meaning. With the prayers of his three Hebrew friends, the Lord revealed the secret to Daniel in a night vision.

Daniel's God-given interpretive abilities were superior to those of the wise men of Babylon; the magicians, astrologers, sorcerers, Chaldeans, and soothsayers. They would work together, each class supplementing the work of the other, to give Nebuchadnezzar a satisfactory solution. Occult practices are an abomination in God's sight and

**DANIEL** DELIVERS THE DREAM AND INTERPRETATION TO **NEBUCHADNEZZAR**.

strictly forbidden to God's children (Deuteronomy 18:9-14). When asked both to tell _and_ interpret the king's dream, the Chaldeans complained, "...There is not a man upon the earth that can show the king's matter... and there is none other that can show it before the king, except the gods, whose dwelling is not with flesh" (Daniel 2:10-11). When Daniel told both the dream and its interpretation, Nebuchadnezzar declared, "...Of a truth _it is_, that

6

your God *is* a God of gods, and a Lord of kings, and a revealer of secrets, seeing thou couldest reveal this secret" (Daniel 2:47). In the letter which the king dispatched to all people, nations, and languages dwelling in all the earth, he distinguished Daniel as one in whom is "the spirit of the holy gods" and called him master of the magicians (Daniel 4:8-9).

In the time of Belshazzar (royal descendant of Nebuchadnezzar), the queen spoke of Daniel: "There is a man in thy kingdom, in whom *is* the spirit of the holy gods; and in the days of thy father light and understanding and wisdom, like the wisdom of the gods, was found in him; whom the king Nebuchadnezzar thy father, the king, *I say*, thy father, made master of the magicians, astrologers, Chaldeans, *and* soothsayers; Forasmuch as an excellent spirit, and knowledge, and understanding, interpreting of dreams, and showing of hard sentences, and dissolving of doubts, were found in the same Daniel..." (Daniel 5:11-12). Daniel's influence is clear. His God-given gifts were superior to those who practiced occult arts. Just as Moses and Aaron had showed the Lord's superior power to the magicians of Egypt (Exodus 7:8-12), Daniel was God's instrument to do the same in Babylon (Daniel 2:27-28).

Complete these sentences.

1.28   The four Hebrew children were probably versed in all the wisdom of a. _____ , as Moses was learned in all the wisdom of b. _____ .

1.29   God gave Daniel the interpretation through a. _____ and
b. _____ .

1.30   Daniel's gift glorifies _____ as the only interpreter of dreams.

1.31   According to Deuteronomy 18, occult practices are an _____ to the Lord.

God alone. Someone given similar abilities to those that Daniel had could easily have become puffed up with pride and taken the credit for them. However, Daniel insisted on giving God the glory in every situation where spiritual gifts were displayed. When recounting his dream to Nebuchadnezzar, he pointed the king's attention to the God that reveals secrets, and refused to take credit for it. He said, "...this secret is not revealed to me for *any* wisdom that I have more than any living..." (Daniel 2:30).

When the king promoted him to leadership of the whole Babylonian province and made him chief of the governors over the wise men, Daniel shared his honor with his three Hebrew friends, for he requested that they also be promoted.

Daniel told the truth in difficult situations, as seen in his second audience with Nebuchadnezzar. In Daniel 4:19, he was disturbed as God gave him the interpretation, for he wished the well being of his king. Daniel had to announce a weighty judgment from God, and after presenting the facts, he solemnly warned Nebuchadnezzar to desist from his sins and iniquities that the days of his tranquillity may be lengthened (Daniel 4:27). Although the king did not immediately heed God's warning, Daniel was daringly honest.

Choose the correct answer.

1.32   Moses and _____ showed the superior power of God to the Egyptians.
    a. Gabriel   d. Daniel
    b. Joseph   e. Hananiah
    c. Aaron

7

1.33   Daniel directed Nebuchadnezzar's attention to the God in heaven that reveals _____ .

    a. wisdom   d. handwriting

    b. secrets   e. truth

    c. mysteries

1.34   The king promoted Daniel and made him chief of the _____ over all the wise men in the whole province of Babylon.

    a. rulers   d. eunuchs

    b. magicians   e. governors

    c. astrologers

Daniel continued to show his honesty during the feast at which he gave an interpretation to Belshazzar. A thousand lords of the Babylonian kingdom were gathered. The ruler and his princes, wives, and concubines drank from sacred vessels taken from the Jerusalem Temple and praised the gods of gold, silver, brass, iron, wood, and stone. God interrupted the king with a message of judgment He wrote on a wall: MENE, MENE, TEKEL, UPHARSIN. When Belshazzar promised Daniel that he would be clothed with scarlet, have a chain of gold about his neck, and be third ruler in the kingdom if he could interpret the handwriting on the wall, he replied, "Let thy gifts be to thyself, and give thy rewards to another; yet I will read the writing unto the king, and make known to him the interpretation" (Daniel 5:17). Daniel did not desire political power or position, but was dependent upon God both to protect and promote him. Before interpreting the handwriting, Daniel delivered a message to this monarch regarding his rebellion against God. He said to the king, "And thou... O Belshazzar, hast not humbled thine heart... But hast lifted up thyself against the Lord of heaven... and the God in whose hand thy breath *is*, and whose *are* all thy ways, hast thou not glorified" (Daniel 5:22-23). Daniel then explained the judgment which was to befall this king and his kingdom that very night. MENE meant "God hath numbered thy kingdom, and finished it"; and, being repeated, it is certain. TEKEL was interpreted "Thou art weighed in the balances and art found wanting." UPHARSIN'S present tense form PERES, signified "Thy Kingdom is divided and has been given to the Medes and Persians." The king was not pleased with these words, but instead of sentencing Daniel to death, he honored him by promoting him to the promised position.

Daniel earned the respect of the monarchs by his character and convictions, and outlived all of them. Maintain humility before the Lord and use the abilities He gives us, giving Him alone credit.

✒️➤ **Match these items.**

1.35	_____ Joseph	a. Daniel's Babylonian name
1.36	_____ Solomon	b. (Hebrew name) thrown into furnace
1.37	_____ Mishael	c. called Daniel *master of the magicians*
1.38	_____ Nebuchadnezzar	d. wisest king of Israel
1.39	_____ Moses	e. interpreted Pharaoh's dreams
1.40	_____ Belshazzar	f. could not read the handwriting on the wall
1.41	_____ Daniel	g. showed God's power to the Egyptian magicians
1.42	_____ Belteshazzar	h. had understanding in all visions and dreams

1.43   By what five names were the wise men of Babylon called?

a. _____   d. _____

b. _____   e. _____

c. _____

1.44   What were the two descriptions of Daniel in Nebuchadnezzar's letter sent to all people, nations, and languages of the world?

a. _____

b. _____

1.45   What were eight different qualities or abilities described by Belshazzar's queen of Daniel?

a. _____   e. _____

b. _____   f. _____

c. _____   g. _____

d. _____   h. _____

1.46   What was Daniel's plea to Nebuchadnezzar after the interpretation of the second dream?

_____

1.47   What were the three accusations Daniel charged Belshazzar with before he interpreted the handwriting on the wall.

a. _____

b. _____

c. _____

1.48   Complete the meaning of the words written on Belshazzar's wall.

a. MENE _____ and finished it

b. TEKEL _____ and art found wanting

c. PERES or UPHARSIN _____

1.49   What were the three rewards promised to Daniel by Belshazzar if he delivered the interpretation of the handwriting on the wall?

a. _____

b. _____

c. _____

1.50   From the viewpoint of a Babylonian reporter covering the feast of Belshazzar, write a 600-word report of the events that occurred.

Submit your report to your teacher for help in evaluation.

Score   _____
Adult check   _____
                   Initial   **Date**

WATCHMAN OF PRAYER

Often, a great leader is marred by nationalistic tendencies, focusing on parochial concerns which prevent him from viewing issues from God's point of view. However, Daniel's concern was also for the Gentile kingdoms of the earth. God made Daniel one of the most superb statesmen of all time. Daniel's lack of concern for himself was due to his total dependence upon God. Daniel's unceasing intercession for Israel throughout a lifetime in a hostile country makes his example worthy of **emulation**.

His unselfish concern. Although he was removed from Judah and taken to Babylon, Daniel was content. As a youth he dedicated himself to the Lord, determined to follow His Law, trusting that God cares for him in all circumstances. Rather than going on a hunger strike that would have endangered the lives of his immediate captors, he was concerned enough about their welfare to offer a creative alternative. When Daniel saw that the lives of all the wise men of Babylon were in danger from the king's decree, he intervened with both Arioch (captain of the guard) and Nebuchadnezzar, to prevent their destruction. When Daniel was rewarded with great gifts and made ruler over Babylon, he requested that Shadrach, Meshach, and Abednego share in his exaltation.

Although he could have justly harbored disdain for his captors (they had brutally besieged his homeland, carried away the sacred vessels and destroyed the Temple), instead, he had a genuine concern for their welfare. When Daniel received the answer concerning the king's second dream, his **solicitude** for the ruler's well-being was clear in his concern and worry over the interpretation. When urged to divulge the matter, he replied, "...My lord, the dream *be* to them that hate thee, and the interpretation thereof to thine enemies" (Daniel 4:19). He then delivered an impassioned speech, entreating him to change his ways in order to avoid the judgment of God.

Daniel's attitude is in stark contrast to the lack of concern shown by the prophet Jonah. Jonah fled to avoid preaching to the heathen nation of Nineveh and later became angry because God spared them when they repented. Daniel's concerns were not nationalistic, but centered around the grace of God.

His continued intercession. Daniel's communion in daily prayer was a main staple of his life. Daniel's prayers did not consist of petitions, but were filled with praise and thanksgiving for God's already adequate provisions. "...(H)e went into his house; and his windows being open in his chamber toward Jerusalem, he kneeled upon his knees three times a day, and prayed, and gave thanks before his God, as he did aforetime" (Daniel 6:10).

Daniel did not pray alone about weighty matters. In Daniel 2, he made his companions completely aware of the dire situation and requested that they pray specifically concerning the secret of the king's dream. When their requests were granted in a night vision, Daniel broke into praise.

The princes and presidents under Darius, governor of Babylon, could find no fault in Daniel, so the princes wanted to trap him by having Darius sign a decree permitting no one to offer a petition to anyone but him for thirty days.

***DANIEL* PRAYING IN THE LION'S DEN.**

10

Knowing about Darius' decree, Daniel continued to openly pray three times a day. When Daniel was cast into the den of lions, the king spent the night fasting for the servant's deliverance. Once Daniel was rescued, Darius made a decree that everyone in his dominion tremble and fear before the God of Daniel "...for he *is* the living God, and steadfast for ever, and his kingdom *that* which shall not be destroyed, and his dominion *shall be even* unto the end. He delivereth and rescueth, and he worketh signs and wonders in heaven and in earth, who hath delivered Daniel from the power of the lions" (Daniel 6:26-27).

During the first year of the reign of Darius the Mede, Daniel recorded the prayer found in Daniel 9. By studying certain books, he understood that the seventy-year-period of captivity spoken of by the prophet Jeremiah was coming to an end. He poured out his heart to God for the restoration to their land. Through prayer and supplications, with fasting, sackcloth, and ashes, Daniel confessed the sin and iniquity of himself and his fathers. Daniel asked the Lord to hear, forgive, hearken, and do what he requested. While he was speaking, the Lord sent his angel, Gabriel, to show him a vision, declaring that Daniel was greatly beloved. He explained that the Lord inclined His ear to hear His servant from the very beginning of his prayer.

In the third year of Cyrus, king of Persia, Daniel mourned and fasted for three full weeks. From the first day, God heard his word and sent forth an angel to minister to him. The prince of Persia withstood the angel for twenty-one days until Michael, one of the chief princes, came to his aid. The one fighting the Lord's messenger could have been an evil angel. After his battle with the prince of Persia and interview with Daniel, the angel returned to fight the prince of Persia a second time and also the prince of Greece.

Match these items.

1.51	_____ Arioch	a. powerful evil angel over kingdom of Grecia
1.52	_____ Darius	b. angel sent to answer Daniel's prayer
1.53	_____ Gabriel	c. captain of Nebuchadnezzar's guard
1.54	_____ Cyrus	d. possibly an evil angel over Persia
1.55	_____ Michael	e. governor of Babylon
1.56	_____ prince of Persia	f. archangel sent to help Gabriel
1.57	_____ Jeremiah	g. prophet who wrote of the seventy-year captivity
1.58	_____ prince of Grecia	h. king of the Persian Empire
1.59	_____ Jonah	i. prophet who did not want to preach to Nineveh

Complete these activities.

1.60　What were seven facts claimed by King Darius about God once Daniel was rescued from the lions?

a. _____

b. _____

c. _____

d. _____

e. _____

f. _____

g. _____

1.61　What five things did Daniel do when he learned of the seventy-year desolation of Jerusalem?

a. _____　　d. _____

b. _____　　e. _____

c. _____

11

Complete these statements.

1.62 Daniel was a. _____ and his thoughts were about his king's well-
b. _____ .

1.36 Daniel's prayers were filled with a. _____ and b. _____ .

1.64 The Lord answered Daniel's prayers and those of his companions by showing him the dream
and interpretation in a _____ at night.

1.65 There was no _____ found in Daniel by the Babylonian wise men.

1.66 After reading about the seventy years, Daniel asked the Lord to a. _____ ,
b. _____ , c. _____ and do that which he requested.

Review the material in this section in preparation for the Self Test. This Self Test will check
your mastery of this particular section. The items missed on this Self Test will indicate specific
areas where restudy is needed for mastery.

SELF TEST 1

Match these items (each answer, 2 points).

1.01	_____ Ashpenaz		a.	Babylonian name of Mishael
1.02	_____ Belteshazzar		b.	king who took people of Judah captive
1.03	_____ Hezekiah		c.	Judah's king who smashed all idols
1.04	_____ Marduk		d.	Daniel's Babylonian name
1.05	_____ Melzar		e.	godly king from whom Daniel may have been descended
1.06	_____ Josiah		f.	prince of Nebuchadnezzar's eunuchs
1.07	_____ Shadrach		g.	Babylonian name of Hananiah
1.08	_____ Abednego		h.	Azariah's Babylonian name
1.09	_____ Nebuchadnezzar		i.	subordinate to Ashpenaz set over Daniel
1.010	_____ Meshach		j.	one of the most important Babylonian gods

Complete these statements (each answer, 3 points).

1.011   The Lord mentioned Daniel and his righteousness with that of Noah and _____ .

1.012   According to 1 Corinthians 10, the heathen Gentile nations sacrificed their food to _____ .

1.013   The book of Daniel is written in both Hebrew and _____ .

1.014   Although he had the prophetic gift, Daniel should be considered a _____ .

1.015   Nebuchadnezzar found Daniel and his three friends ten times better than all the king's magicians and _____ .

1.016   Prophets received instruction from the Lord through dreams and _____ .

1.017   Daniel was _____ in his service to his king and God.

1.018   Occult practices are an _____ in God's eyes. (Deuteronomy 18)

1.019   After he learned of the seventy-year period, Daniel prayed and asked the Lord to hear _____ , hearken, and do.

Choose the correct answer (each answer, 2 points).

1.020   In present Hebrew Bibles, the book of Daniel is included among the _____ .
   a. Prophets   c. Hagiographa
   b. Septuagint   d. Writings

1.021   Nebuchadnezzar promoted Daniel to make him chief of the _____ .
   a. eunuchs   c. rulers
   b. magicians   d. governors

1.022   The four Hebrew children were versed in all the wisdom of Babylon, as Moses had been in the wisdom of _____ .
   a. Persia   c. Media
   b. Egypt   d. Israel

13

Complete these activities (each answer, 3 points).

1.023   List three changes made to the life of Daniel and his friends in order to obliterate their heritage.

a. _____

b. _____

c. _____

1.024   Name three powerful prophets of God in Judah when Daniel was young.

a. _____

b. _____

c. _____

1.025   What were the five names given to the wise men of Babylon?

a. _____   d. _____

b. _____   e. _____

c. _____

1.026   What were Daniel's five qualities as described by the queen to Belshazzar?

a. _____   d. _____

b. _____   e. _____

c. _____

Answer *true* **or** *false* (each answer, 1 point).

1.027   _____   The Babylonian Captivity lasted for seventy years.

1.028   _____   Daniel complained bitterly because he was taken captive.

1.029   _____   Daniel offered a creative alternative to avoid eating defiled food.

1.030   _____   Daniel delighted in giving Nebuchadnezzar God's judgment.

1.031   _____   Daniel prayed three times a day toward Jerusalem.

1.032   _____   Darius signed a petition to prevent people from petitioning anyone but him for thirty days.

1.033   _____   King Darius fasted all night when Daniel was in the lions' den.

1.034   _____   The prince of Persia withstood Gabriel in spiritual battle for fourteen days.

87 / 109

Score
Adult check _____

                                     Initial   **Date**

BIBLE

LIFEPAC TEST

84 / 105

Name _____

Date _____

Score _____

BIBLE 1207: LIFEPAC TEST

Match these items (each answer, 2 points).

1. _____ Jeremiah
2. _____ Josiah
3. _____ Hezekiah
4. _____ Belshazzar
5. _____ bear
6. _____ lion
7. _____ Darius
8. _____ Nebuchadnezzar
9. _____ he-goat
10. _____ Cyrus

a. king who took people of Judah captive
b. prophet whom Daniel probably heard as a boy
c. king who held a blasphemous feast
d. godly king who smashed Judah's idols
e. symbolic of Medo-Persian Empire
f. king from whom Daniel may be descended
g. symbolic of Grecian Empire
h. symbolic of the Babylonian Empire
i. king under whom Daniel was rescued from lions
j. last king under whom Daniel served

Complete these statements (each answer, 3 points).

11. Daniel's name, language, education, and _____ were changed when he became captive in Babylon.

12. Daniel held important positions of influence in the Babylonian, _____ , and Persian Empires.

13. Daniel was made chief of the _____ over all the wise men in the province of Babylon.

14. The four words written on the wall at Belshazzar's feast were MENE, _____ , UPHARSIN, or PERES.

15. After reading the prophecy of Jeremiah, Daniel humbled himself by prayer and supplications with (three things).

16. The fourth beast symbolizes the _____ .

17. We saints are _____ and priests for God.

Choose the correct answer (each answer, 2 points).

18. The lion corresponds with the head of _____ of Nebuchadnezzar's dream.
    a. brass
    b. iron
    c. gold
    d. clay
    e. silver

19. The fourth beast of Daniel's vision symbolizes the _____ Empire.
    a. Grecian
    b. Medo-Persian
    c. Babylonian
    d. Roman
    e. Maccabean

20. The Lord sent the angel _____ to give Daniel revelation.
    a. Michael
    b. Ulai
    c. Lydia
    d. Gabriel
    e. Lucifer

1

21. The prophecy of the seventy weeks centers around ____ .
   a. calculations   d. antichrist
   b. dates   e. figures
   c. Messiah

22. The king of Persia who was rich above all was ____ .
   a. Cyrus   d. Cambyses
   b. Xerxes   e. Smerdis
   c. Xenophon

Complete these items (each answer, 3 points).

23. List the three periods into which the seventy weeks are divided.
   a. _____   c. _____
   b. _____

24. Name the four heads of the leopard representing Alexander's kingdom after it was divided.
   a. _____   c. _____
   b. _____   d. _____

25. State four requirements of Nebuchadnezzar concerning the young men who were to be trained for his service.
   a. _____   c. _____
   b. _____   d. _____

26. Name four qualities found in Daniel, according to the queen's description of him to Belshazzar.
   a. _____   c. _____
   b. _____   d. _____

NOTES

II. VISIONS

Like Revelation in the New Testament, portions of Daniel are **apocalyptic** literature. The revelations found in Daniel, delivered in dreams and visions, contain an abundance of imagery and symbolism. Imagery is used in several Old Testament books such as Isaiah, Joel, Zechariah, Psalms, and Amos, but no other prophetical writing speaks with the same fullness and definitiveness as Daniel does concerning the Gentile nations in relation to God's elect.

Judah was in captivity and under the judgment of the LORD, and it raised many questions about the nation's future. Through these visions, the Lord showed that He had not cast His people off forever and would not leave them scattered among the nations. God fulfilled His promises in sending the Messiah to redeem them. Although the heathen nations rose one upon another and became politically powerful, all are subject to the sovereign control of God. God's people endured great persecution at the hands of the heathen, but at the appointed time, God established His own everlasting kingdom.

SECTION OBJECTIVES

Review these objectives. When you have completed this section, you should be able to:

5. Describe the vision of the four beasts.
6. Describe the vision of the ram and the he-goat.
7. Outline the revelation of seventy sevens.
8. Describe the vision of the mighty kings.

VOCABULARY

Study these words to enhance your learning success in this section.

apocalyptic

atrocities

Hellenize

ignominious

myriad

 Read Daniel 7.

THE FOUR BEASTS

The vision of the four beasts was given to Daniel in the first year of the reign of Belshazzar, when the power and glory of the Babylonian Empire had begun to wane. The vision was very similar to Nebuchadnezzar's dream, which was given when Babylon was at the height of its power. Both deal with four great earthly kingdoms which would follow one another in succession.

The vision. Daniel had a divinely imposed dream, and when he awoke, he wrote down its contents. In the dream, the four winds of heaven burst forth upon the Great Sea, and as a result, four distinct beasts rose up from the water. The first beast looked like a lion, but had the wings of an eagle. This beast was lifted up, stood on two feet and was given a man's heart (Daniel 7:4).

The second beast was like a bear; it was raised up on one side and had three ribs in its mouth between its teeth. This beast was told "...Arise, devour much flesh" (Daniel 7:5).

A third beast arose, like a leopard, having four wings of a bird on its back and four heads. Dominion was given to this one as well (Daniel 7:6).

The fourth beast was dreadful, terrible, exceedingly strong, and had iron teeth. This beast devoured, broke in pieces, and trampled everything under its feet. This creature seems to have defied description (Daniel 7:7). It had ten horns, three of which were plucked up by the roots by a little horn coming up among the ten. This small horn had eyes like a man and a mouth speaking pompous words ("great things" KJV, Daniel 7:8).

As Daniel continued to look upon this little horn's activities, a heavenly scene broke upon his view. The Ancient of Days sat, having a garment white as snow and hair like pure wool. His throne was like flames of fire and its wheels as burning fire. A river of fire was flowing forth from before Him, a thousand thousands ministered unto Him while **myriads** stood before Him. The court sat, and the books were opened for judgment. While Daniel beheld the vision of judgment, he continued to hear the presumptuous words of the little horn; and as he watched, the beast was slain, his body was destroyed, being devoured in the fiery stream coming forth from God. Although the lives of the first three beasts were extended for a time and a season, their dominion was taken away. At the conclusion of the vision, one like the Son of Man came with the clouds of heaven and was presented unto the Ancient of Days. To Him was given dominion, glory, and a kingdom so that all people, nations, and languages served him. This dominion is everlasting and His kingdom shall not be destroyed. This vision was the first great one given to Daniel about God's kingdom set up against the kingdoms of this world.

Match these items.

2.1	_____ apocalyptic	a.	the first beast
2.2	_____ Belshazzar	b.	literary genre marked by heavy imagery and symbolism
2.3	_____ had ten horns	c.	the second beast
2.4	_____ winged lion	d.	the fourth beast
2.5	_____ bear	e.	Daniel's vision came in the first year of his reign
2.6	_____ leopard	f.	the third beast
2.7	_____ Nebuchadnezzar	g.	a term used to represent God the Father
2.8	_____ Ancient of Days	h.	had a dream which corresponds to Daniel's vision

Answer *true* **or** *false*.

2.9 _____ The vision of the four beasts came to Daniel in the second year of Nebuchadnezzar's reign.

2.10 _____ Daniel was wide awake when this vision came to him.

2.11 _____ Portions of the book of Daniel are apocalyptic literature.

2.12 _____ No imagery nor symbolism was used in the visions of Daniel.

2.13 _____ The fourth beast looked like a particular animal.

2.14 _____ The leopard or panther had four wings and four heads.

2.15 _____ The beasts were given extensions to their dominion.

The meaning. The four winds (Daniel 8:8; 11:4; Zechariah 2:6; and 6:5) seem to symbolize God's heavenly power. The Great Sea upon which the winds burst forth is generally thought to signify mankind, humanity, or the nations of the world (Revelation 17:1 and 15). The Lord dictates the nations of the world and their actions. The imagery employed is that of tumultuous waves of invading armies overriding countries without control (Isaiah 17:12-14).

The first beast corresponds to the head of gold in Daniel 2, and symbolizes the Babylonian Empire, particularly as represented by the reign of Nebuchadnezzar. In many places in the Scriptures, this king of Babylon is compared with a lion and an eagle (Jeremiah 4:7; 49:19; 50:17, and 44; Lamentations 4:19; Habakkuk 1:8; and Ezekiel 17:3 and 12). In Daniel's vision, the wings were plucked so the beast could no longer fly over the earth as a conqueror or hover over it as a ruler. The beast was neither destroyed nor removed from the earth, but was raised up to stand on two feet, having its nature changed to that of a man. This humanizing process is a reference to Nebuchadnezzar's humiliation, which resulted in a more humane rule when he was restored to the headship of the Babylonian Empire (Daniel 4:28-37). This empire lasted from about 609 to 539 B.C.

The strength and fierceness of the second beast was symbolized by his bear-like appearance. The bear was raised on one side, signifying that its feet on one side were raised, ready to move forward. This beast represented the double-sided Medo-Persian Empire ready to march forward in conquest. History reveals that the Medo-Persians ruled from 539 to 330 B.C.

The third beast, looking like a leopard or panther, denoted the Grecian Empire of Alexander the Great. The swiftness and lightning-like nature of Alexander's conquests are well represented by this agile animal with two pairs of wings. The four heads of this beast referred to the four generals who divided Alexander's empire: Ptolemy, Seleucus, Philip, and Antigonus. This beast corresponds with the brass belly and thighs of the image in Daniel 2. Under Alexander the Great, the Grecian Empire lasted from 330 to 220 B.C. Upon his death, the empire was divided among his four generals and continued in diverse forms until 63 B.C.

The powerfully destructive fourth beast corresponds with the iron legs and feet of the image in Nebuchadnezzar's dream. This beast's ability to conquer was indicated by the iron teeth which crushed and devoured, leaving debris that was stamped under its feet. No creatures were combined to picture the crushing rage or stupendous power of this fourth beast, which represented the Roman Empire. The universal conquests of Rome and its unequaled ability to subdue its conquered territories are well represented. The Roman Empire came to full power in 63 B.C.

The ten horns represented kings or kingdoms that arose during the empire's existence. This later phase accords well with the ten iron and clay toes of the image of Daniel 2. Arising out of the ten horns was a little horn which destroyed three of the others and spoke as a pompous windbag.

Chapter 2	Chapter 7	Kingdoms	Chapter 8
Head of Gold	Lion	Babylon 609-539 B.C.	
Arms of Silver	Bear	Medo-Persia 539-331 B.C.	Ram
Sides of Brass	Leopard	Greece 331-165 B.C.	He-goat
Legs of Iron	Nondescript Beast	Rome 63 B.C.- (officially) 476 A.D.	

Some believe the little horn refers to the one spoken of by Paul in 2 Thessalonians 2:3-4:

"Let no man deceive you by any means: for *that day shall not come*, except there come a falling away first, and that man of sin be revealed, the son of perdition; Who opposeth and exalteth himself above all that is called God, or that is worshipped; so that he as God sitteth in the temple of God, showing himself that he is God."

The fourth beast portrays a remarkable record of the Roman Empire, whose leader, the Caesars slaughtered the saints, set up their pagan standards in the temple and proclaimed themselves as Lord (God).

The final, climactic scene of the vision represents the presentation of the Lord Jesus Christ (Son of Man) to the Father (Ancient of Days). Surrounded by the holy angels and saints of all the ages, Christ received the dominion and glory of God's kingdom. The conquest of the ages culminates in claiming the kingdoms of this world for God, who reigns forever and ever (Revelation 11:15). Because we saints are kings and priests for God (Revelation 1:6 and 5:10), we share equally with Christ in His kingdom as heirs of God and joint heirs with Jesus Christ (Romans 8:17 and James 2:5).

 Complete these activities.

2.16 Briefly describe these aspects of the vision of the first beast.

a. appearance _____

_____

b. corresponds to _____ of Nebuchadnezzar's dream

c. symbolizes _____

2.17   Briefly describe these aspects of the vision of the second beast.

       a. appearance _____

           _____

       b. corresponds to _____ of Nebuchadnezzar's dream

       c. symbolizes _____

2.18   Briefly describe these aspects of the vision of the third beast.

       a. appearance _____

           _____

       b. corresponds to _____ of Nebuchadnezzar's dream

       c. symbolizes _____

2.19   Briefly describe these aspects of the vision of the fourth beast.

       a. appearance _____

       b. corresponds to _____ of Nebuchadnezzar's dream

       c. symbolizes _____

2.20   What did Christ receive as surrounded by the holy angels and saints of all ages?

       _____

       _____

2.21   What are we for God as we share equally in His Kingdom?

       _____

       _____

 Read Daniel 8.

THE RAM AND THE HE-GOAT

THE RAM AND THE HE-GOAT

Daniel's second vision came two years after the first, during the third year of Belshazzar's reign. Because no mention is made in this passage to Daniel sleeping, some students assume that Daniel was awake when he received it.

The vision. In the vision, Daniel saw himself in Elam province in Shushan palace by the Ulai river. This city, also called Susa, dates from 3000 B.C. and was Elam's capital. The city came under the control of various empires (Assyrian, Babylonian, and Medo-Persian) and continued to be inhabited until the Middle Ages. Susa was the chief capital of the Persian Empire and is the setting of the book of Esther (Esther 1:2). The Ulai was a nine hundred feet wide artificial canal, passing by Susa on the northeast side (Daniel 8:2).

By the river, Daniel saw a ram with two high horns, the last one being higher than the other. This ram was pushing and butting his way west, north, and south. No other beast could stand before him. The ram did as he pleased and increased his greatness. As Daniel pondered the ram, a he-goat with a conspicuous horn between his eyes came from the west across all the earth, never touching the ground.

The he-goat attacked the ram in wrath, broke his two horns, cast him to the ground, and trampled him. When the he-goat became powerful, the great horn was broken, and four horns took its place, pointing towards the four winds of heaven. Out of one of these horns came forth a little horn which extended toward the southeast to Palestine. This horn became great and caused some of the host of heaven and the stars to fall to the earth where it trampled them. The little horn took away the sacrifices and cast down the sanctuary. An army was given to the horn to oppose the sacrifices, truth was cast to the ground, and he prospered (Daniel 8:11-12).

The meaning. The ram was an emblem of princely power (Ezekiel 34:17; 39:18) and, according to Daniel 8:20, referred to the kings of Media and Persia. The horn which grew higher than the other represented the quick conquests of Darius and Cyrus and pointed to where the Persian Empire made the greatest conquests. The Persians ruled Palestine, Asia Minor, and Egypt from 539 to 330 B.C.

The he-goat represented the Grecian Empire, and the notable horn between the goat's eyes was Alexander the Great (Daniel 8:21). His conquests were extremely rapid, symbolized by the goat not touching the earth. The breaking of the two horns and trampling of the ram by the he-goat depicted the utter destruction of the Persian Empire. Alexander's early death was symbolized in the vision by the breaking of the great horn at the height of his conquests. The four horns represented the four kingdoms into which Alexander's Empire was divided: Macedonia under Cassander, Thrace and Asia Minor under Lysimachus, Syria under Seleucus, and Egypt under Ptolemy. The Grecian Empire was eventually dispersed to the four winds. It lasted from 330 to 220 B.C.

The little horn is Antiochus IV Epiphanes, the great persecutor of God's people. Antiochus pushed his conquests to Egypt on the south, Armenia on the east, and toward Canaan, the pleasant land which lies between the two (Isaiah 19:23-25; Jeremiah 3:19, and Daniel 11:16,41). This little horn must not be confused with the little horn of Daniel 7, which came up from the fourth beast, the Roman Empire. The host of heaven, which Antiochus dispersed and cast to the ground are the saints of God, pictured as stars in Daniel 12:3 and Jeremiah 33:22. The **atrocities** of Antiochus against God's saints were actually attacks against the Lord Himself. After invading Judah, Antiochus stopped the offerings and sacrifices in the sanctuary. He commanded their religious culture be destroyed. Although he did not tear down the Temple, he desecrated it by erecting an altar to Zeus and sacrificing a pig on it. Antiochus cast down God's worship, killed many Jews, and pursued a program of radical **Hellenization**.

The voices Daniel heard speaking in this vision questioned the length of the transgression of desolation during which the sanctuary and Jewish saints would be trodden under foot. The answer given was "...Unto two thousand and three hundred days..." (Daniel 8:14). A Hebrew reader recognizes this period as lasting a full 2,300 days. This number perhaps referred to the abominations of Antiochus which lasted approximately six years. The corruption began about 171 B.C., and the desecration of the Temple took place in 167 B.C. After Antiochus IV's death in 164 B.C., the sanctuary was reconstructed on the twenty-fifth day of Chisleu (December 14, 164 B.C.), exactly three years after its desecration. John 10:22 referred to the feast that accompanied that great event as the feast of dedication currently known as Chaunukkah.

The interpretation came through Gabriel at the command of God. The content of the prophecy was confined to the time of the indignation (Daniel 8:19), when God gave up His people to punishment because of their iniquities. The appearance of Antiochus IV proved that they were near the end of the period of discipline and that the Messiah was soon to come. Gabriel did emphasize the power of Antiochus IV, but indicated that it was the providence of God that gave him his might. Antiochus IV was proud, crafty and cunning, using deceit to prosper. The time of "peace" was a time of false security when the conqueror unexpectedly attacked his prey. The Prince of princes is the LORD Himself, as He is called the Prince of the Host in Daniel 8:11. Daniel was told by Gabriel to seal or preserve the prophecy because it was for a long time in the future.

The effect of this vision on Daniel was so great that he became sick for several days. Even after he arose and attended to the business of the king, he was still astonished and perplexed. Because the vision concerned future events, Daniel had difficulty understanding and comprehending it.

Choose the correct answer.

2.22   Daniel's second vision of the ram and he-goat came during the _____ year of Belshazzar's reign.

a. second   d. first

b. fifth   e. fourth

c. third

2.23   The city of _____ or Susa was the chief capital of the Persian Empire.

a. Babylon   d. Elam

b. Media   e. Shushan

c. Ulai

2.24   The period during which the Jews were persecuted was described by Gabriel as the _____ .

a. wrath   d. fury

b. indignation   e. heat

c. penance

2.25   Daniel was told to _____ the prophetic vision because it was for a long time in the future.

a. destroy   d. abandon

b. explain   e. seal

c. tell

2.26   The content of the vision and the circumstances surrounding the giving of it were so powerful that Daniel was _____ for several days.

a. well   d. elated

b. excited   e. disgusted

c. sick

Complete these statements.

2.27   In the vision, Daniel saw himself in the palace of a. _____ by the river b. _____ in the province of c. _____ .

2.28   The ram in the vision did not push _____ -ward.

2.29   The Temple at Jerusalem was desecrated by Antiochus IV Epiphanes when he sacrificed a _____ on the altar to Zeus.

2.30   The Lord commanded the angel _____ to reveal to Daniel the interpretation of the vision.

20

Match these items.

2.31 _____ Esther

2.32 _____ Ulai

2.33 _____ ram

2.34 _____ Susa

2.35 _____ Alexander the Great

2.36 _____ 171-164 B.C.

2.37 _____ Antiochus IV Epiphanes

2.38 _____ Belshazzar

a. Daniel saw the vision in the third year of his reign

b. capital of Elam

c. evil ruler who desecrated the Temple

d. time of the abominations of Antiochus IV

e. emblem of princely power

f. ruler of the Grecian Empire

g. speaks of Shushan the palace

h. artificial canal nine hundred feet wide

Complete these activities.

2.39 Briefly describe these aspects of Daniel's second vision.

a. ram _____

_____

_____

b. symbolizes _____

c. he-goat _____

_____

_____

_____

_____

d. symbolizes _____

2.40 Indicate the symbolic meaning of the following items.

a. the goat's notable horn _____

b. the four horns _____

c. the little horn of Daniel 8 _____

d. the host of heaven _____

2.41 Name the four kingdoms into which the Grecian Empire was divided and their individual leaders.

a. _____ : _____

b. _____ : _____

c. _____ : _____

d. _____ : _____

2.42 List eleven facts given about Antiochus IV Epiphanes in Daniel 8:23-25.

a. _____

b. _____

c. _____

d. _____

e. _____

f. _____

g. _____

h. _____

i. _____

j. _____

k. _____

2.43   What is the meaning of the 2,300 days of Daniel 8:14?

_____

_____

_____

 Read Daniel 9.

THE SEVENTY WEEKS

Daniel chapter 9, is one of the more perplexing passages in the Bible and has been subject to a variety of interpretations. This revelation is given by Gabriel in response to Daniel's prayer during the first year of Darius (Daniel 9:1). The revelation occurs after Daniel studied the description of the seventy-year period of the desolation, as given by Jeremiah (Daniel 9:2).

The vision. After Daniel confessed the sins of the Hebrew nation (Daniel 9:4-19), the Lord gave him this revelation. *Seventy weeks* of remaining judgement were decreed by God upon His people and Jerusalem. The reason for this period has three negative and three positive aspects. The negative aspects include restraining transgression, completion of sin, and covering iniquity. The positive aspects include bringing in everlasting righteousness, sealing the vision and prophecy, and anointing the Most Holy.

Daniel 9:25-27 describes a division of these seventy sevens into three particular parts: seven weeks, sixty-two weeks and one week. Daniel 9:25-27 states:

> Know therefore and understand, *that* from the going forth of the commandment to restore and to build Jerusalem unto the Messiah the Prince *shall be* seven weeks, and threescore and two weeks: the street shall be built again, and the wall, even in troublous times.
>
> And after threescore and two weeks shall Messiah be cut off, but not for himself: and the people of the prince that shall come shall destroy the city and the sanctuary; and the end thereof *shall be* with a flood, and unto the end of the war desolations are determined.
>
> And he shall confirm the covenant with many for one week: and in the midst of the week he shall cause the sacrifice and the oblation to cease, and for the overspreading of abominations he shall make *it* desolate, even until the consummation, and that determined shall be poured upon the desolate.

The meaning. Three main interpretations have been advanced for this difficult passage.

The first is the Church's historical interpretation (known as the *covenantal* position), which regards this passage as a prophecy relating to the first advent of Christ, with His death as the central issue. Christ makes a covenant of grace with His redeemed, through His blood, ending the old covenant sacrifices. The prophecy concludes with the destruction of Jerusalem by the Romans in A.D. 70.

The *dispensational* interpretation views the beginning of the seventy sevens is seen as being 444 B.C., the twentieth year of Artaxerxes. The seven 'sevens' (weeks) at the start refer to the forty-nine years of rebuilding Jerusalem's walls. The sixty-two began immediately thereafter and extended to the triumphal entry of Christ into Jerusalem, following which the Messiah was "cut off" to the Jews. According to this view, because national Israel did not proclaim Christ as the Messiah, the promises of Daniel 9:24 never happened. In this interpretation, great time gap (more than nineteen hundred years) follows this sixty-ninth week because God postponed the seventieth week; all due to the Jews' failure to recognize Christ. During this time, God abandons Israel in favor of offering the Gospel to the Gentiles (our present condition). When God once more chooses to deal with Israel, the seventieth week will begin; and a great "Roman" leader (antichrist) will appear pretending to befriend the Jews. This leader will make a seven-year covenant with the nation of Israel. Either in the midst of this week, or after three and one-half years, he will break the covenant and force Jewish worship to cease. The "great tribulation" will be ushered in for the following three and one-half years.

A third view may be termed the *antichristic* interpretation. In this view, the weeks are only symbolic numbers. After the seventy years of exile, the people of God are brought to salvation until the consummation of time. This period is divided into three parts. The first of seven sevens begins with the edict of Cyrus for the rebuilding of the Temple and extends to the Advent of Christ. Following this first period, the period of sixty-two sevens occurs. The "returning" and "rebuilding" during this period figuratively expresses the preaching of the Gospel. Much affliction occurs at this time and continues until the Anointed is "cut off." In the period following, all influence of the Messiah is lost; and He no longer has any power or influence over the world. A counterfeit comes to take His position, a wicked prince whose people destroys God's city and sanctuary and brings war and destruction. This antichrist dominates the last seven of the sevens. Finally, his domination is brought to a close by the absolute consummation of all things.-

---

Answer *true* or *false*.

2.44 _____ It is unclear which interpretation is true.

2.45 _____ Daniel had this vision revealed in the first year of Cyrus.

2.46 _____ The vision was sent through Gabriel in answer to Daniel's prayer.

2.47 _____ The prophecy in this passage is centered around God's people.

2.48 _____ The final termination of the seventy sevens is clearly stated.

2.49 _____ The rebuilding of Jerusalem might be one of the things discussed in the prophecy.

2.50 _____ The antichrist is referred to in every interpretation of this prophecy.

Complete these activities.

2.51 What are the three periods into which the seventy sevens are divided (Daniel 9:25-27)?

a. _____   c. _____

b. _____

2.52 Briefly outline the interpretation which you believe best reflects the facts of the passage. Why you agree with that interpretation? If a better interpretation exists, outline it and give your reasons for preferring it.

a. interpretation: _____

_____

_____

_____

_____

_____

_____

b. reasons: _____

_____

_____

_____

_____

_____

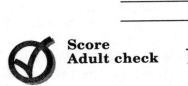

Score
Adult check _____

Initial   Date

 Read Daniel 10, 11, and 12.

THE MIGHTY KINGS

The vision of the kings, given to Daniel in the third year of Cyrus, occurred after he had fasted and prayed for three weeks. Such intense prayer and fasting drained Daniel of all his strength and caused him to lie flat on his face until the angel Gabriel raised him up and strengthened him to receive the revelation. In view of the account of the warfare in which the glorious "person" was engaged (Daniel 10:20), he may be the angel Gabriel. Gabriel related how he had previously worked with Michael in the overthrow of Babylon, which ushered in the Medo-Persian Empire.

The vision. In the vision, Daniel is told that three kings arose from Persia, (Daniel 11:2) but a fourth was far richer than all others. Once he grew strong through his riches, he aroused all against the kingdom of Greece. A mighty king then ruled with great power and in accord to his own will (Daniel 11:3). His kingdom was broken and divided to the four winds of heaven, but not to his posterity. Daniel 11:4 states, "...his kingdom shall be plucked up, even for others beside those." Wars between the subsequent kings of the South and North were fought in order to control Palestine. Next, a despised ruler came in unawares and took hold of the kingdom through intrigues. This person made two expeditions to the South and returned a third time to rage against the holy covenant, giving regard to those who abandoned it. He profaned the sanctuary, removed the sacrifices, and established an abomination. A king is described who exalted and magnified himself against God. The king spoke against God, and prospered until the period of wrath ended. At the end, the southern king went against this mighty king, and the northern king stormed against him. He came into the land of the delight and ruled over the deposits of gold and silver and over all the desired things of Egypt (Daniel 11:42-43). He planted the tents of his pavilion between the sea and the mountain of the delight of holiness. Finally, "...he shall come to his end, and none shall help him" (Daniel 11:45).

Daniel 12 depicts the deliverance of Israel and the consummation of all things. This is a time of great distress, after which will come a resurrection and eternal rewards.

After Daniel was told to seal up the prophecy, two other angels appeared (Daniel 12:5). These angels asked about the length of time of the wondrous things and were told it consisted of a time, times, and half time. When Daniel questioned the angel further, he was told that the words are sealed until the time of the end. Although many believers were to be purified and refined, the wicked continued to do wickedly. Daniel 12:10 states, "...none of the wicked shall understand; but the wise shall understand." A final word of comfort and assurance was given to Daniel in the closing words of the book (Daniel 12:13).

Answer *true* or *false*.

2.53 _____ The vision of the kings was given to Daniel in the fifth year of Darius.

2.54 _____ Gabriel worked with Michael in the overthrow of Babylon.

2.55 _____ The fourth king of Daniel's vision became weak through his wealth.

2.56 _____ The "despised one" profaned the sanctuary.

2.57 _____ The wicked continued to do wickedly.

Answer this question.

2.58   What was the purpose of the last verse of the book of Daniel?

The meaning. Cyrus the Persian was the reigning king reigning when this passage was written. The three rulers following him were Cambyses (529-522 B.C.), Smerdis (522-521 B.C.), and Darius Hystaspis (521-486 B.C.). The fourth ruler, who was rich above all is undoubtedly Xerxes (486-465 B.C.). Xerxes spent much of his treasures establishing and maintaining a large army. The mighty king is Alexander the Great, who was only thirty-three years of age when he died in Babylon.

Although the fourfold division of his kingdom did not occur *immediately* after his death, the kingdom was subsequently divided into four sections. Alexander had two sons, Hercules and Alexander, but they were assassinated shortly after their father's death. At first, Aridaeus was made king and his twelve generals divided the spoils of the empire among themselves. Later the fourfold division emerged, and Alexander's empire was dispersed.

The king of the South was Ptolemy *Soter*, one of Alexander's generals who ruled Egypt from 322 to 305 B.C. The prince was probably Seleucus, another of Alexander's officers who had Babylonia taken from him by Antigonus. In 312 B.C., after P. Soter appointed Seleucus as his general, he took back Babylonia. Seleucus eventually became king, and his dynasty exceeded that of the Ptolemy, reaching from Phrygia to Indus. The alliances between the South and the North were made by Ptolemy *Philadelphus*, Soter's successor, with Antiochus II, Seleucus' successor. P. Philadelphus' daughter Berenice was brought to Antiochus II to be his bride. Two years later, P. Philadelphus died, so Antiochus II divorced Berenice and took back his former wife Laodice, who had borne him two sons. Due to Antiochus II's instability, his wife poisoned him and encouraged her son, Seleucus Callinicus, to murder Berenice and her child, so he would gain the throne unchallenged. These facts agree with the language employed in the revelation through Gabriel.

Then, Berenice's brother Ptolemy *Euergetes* (Egypt's third Ptolemy) came to power. He waged war against the king of the North and killed Laodice. He was very successful and highly acclaimed in Egypt. About 240 B.C., when the Northern King, Seleucus Callinicus, attempted to come against him, P. Euergetes handed him a sound defeat.

Seleucus Callinicus' sons, Seleucus Ceraunus and Antiochus III the Great, are also referred to in the prophecy. Seleucus Ceraunus became king, but died in battle in Asia Minor; Antiochus III the Great became the new ruler of the North. He conquered Phoenicia and Palestine and established his empire in Gaza. The enraged king of the South is perhaps the successor to P. Euergetes, Ptolemy *Philopator*, who defeated Antiochus III the Great at Raphia, but did not press his advantage.

Thirteen years later, Antiochus III came against Egypt when P. Philopator's son was only four years old. Antiochus III was supported by Philip of Macedon and a group of misguided Jews who took his side thinking they were fulfilling prophecies. The reference to taking a fortified city may pertain to Sidon or Gaza, the Palestinian domain of Antiochus III.

Later, Antiochus III betrothed his daughter Cleopatra to the young Ptolemy, hoping to destroy his enemy. However, she sided with her new husband. Antiochus III the Great was subsequently defeated by a magistrate (Lucius Asiaticus) after conquering many of the islands and coastlands of the Mediterranean. Antiochus died in **ignominious** shame, soundly humiliated before his death. Seleucus Philopator succeeded Antiochus III and sent his prime minister, Heliodorus, to seize the money of the Temple treasury in Jerusalem, but he failed. Seleucus was mysteriously (poisoned by Heliodorus?) removed from power.

In Daniel 11:21, the scene changes to the rise of Antiochus IV Epiphanes, the king of the North and great persecutor of the Jews. Some scholars place a double reference to him and "the antichrist" in this passage. The language could be applied to the end of history. He had no reverence for any god (Daniel 11:36), which was not true of Antiochus IV; however, this is true of the antichrist because he magnifies himself above all gods. After hearing that his governor Lysias had been overthrown in Israel and that the altar of the Lord had been set up again in the Holy City, Antiochus IV was terrified and fell sick, dying in dismay.

Those believing this is an antichristic passage believe history's last battle is depicted in Daniel 11:39-43.

The king of the South will come against "the antichrist." His forces overflow Palestine, but the enemies of Israel, Edom, Moab, and Ammon will escape his wrath. Egypt (representing the powers resisting the antichrist) will not escape; and the antichrist will rule over the gold, silver, and all desired things of his enemies. His end comes, troubled by rebellions in the East and North (Daniel 11:44), in territory inhabited by God's people, with no one to help him (Daniel 11:45). This view is common among those who hold to the dispensational or antichristic interpretation of Daniel 9.

Michael the archangel protects God's people. He will deliver only those whose names are written in "the book" (Daniel 12:1). The dead will awake. The wicked will be put to shame and everlasting contempt, while the wise shine forever (Daniel 12:3). Daniel was told to seal up the prophecy until the time of the end (Daniel 12:4), when "...many shall run to and fro, and knowledge shall be increased." In answer to a question of the angelic beings (Daniel 12:6), we are told that the length of time of these wonders is the same as given in Daniel 7:25, "...for a time, times, and an half..." When the power of the "holy people" is shattered, the prophecy is complete. The angel told Daniel that the words were sealed (Daniel 12:8).

Only that which is necessary is revealed for our learning, and many mysteries will remain sealed (Ephesians 2:7), "That in the ages to come he might show the exceeding riches of his grace in *his* kindness toward us through Christ Jesus."

Match these items.

2.59	_____ Hercules	a. daughter of Antiochus III betrothed to Ptolemy
2.60	_____ Aridaeus	b. fortified city taken by Antiochus III
2.61	_____ Antigonus	c. son of Alexander the Great
2.62	_____ Berenice	d. first wife of Antiochus II
2.63	_____ Laodice	e. prime minister of Seleucus Philopator
2.64	_____ Sidon	f. appointed king after Alexander the Great's death
2.65	_____ Cleopatra	g. Ptolemy's daughter who married Antiochus II
2.66	_____ Lucius Asiaticus	h. took Babylonia from Seleucus
2.67	_____ Heliodorus	i. magistrate who defeated Antiochus III the Great

Complete these activities.

2.68 Name five kings of Persia mentioned in this section in order of their reigns.

a. _____   d. _____

b. _____   e. _____

c. _____

2.69 List the kings of the North in the order of their rule, beginning with Seleucus.

a. Seleucus   e. _____

b. _____   f. _____

c. _____   g. _____

d. _____

2.70 List the kings of the South, in the order of their rule, beginning with Ptolemy Soter.

a. Ptolemy Soter   d. Ptolemy _____

b. Ptolemy _____   e. Ptolemy _____

c. Ptolemy _____

2.71   On a separate sheet of paper, write as many points as possible from Daniel 11:21-45 that describe the activities of Antiochus VI Epiphanes. Which of these passages (if any) do you believe refer to the antichrist? Organize a discussion or debate on these two people, pooling the opinions from the student's papers.

Score
Adult check _____
                      Initial   Date

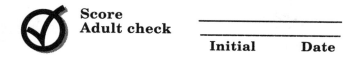

Before you take this last Self Test, you may want to do one or more of these self checks.

1. _____ Read the objectives. Determine if you can do them.

2. _____ Restudy the material related to any objectives that you cannot do.

3. _____ Use the SQ3R study procedure to review the material:
   a. **S**can the sections.
   b. **Q**uestion yourself again (review the questions you wrote initially).
   c. **R**ead to answer your questions.
   d. **R**ecite the answers to yourself.
   e. **R**eview areas you didn't understand.

4. _____ Review all activities and Self Tests, writing a correct answer for each wrong answer.

Match these items (each answer, 2 points).

2.01	_____ Heliodorus	a. son of Alexander the Great
2.02	_____ Cleopatra	b. prime minister of Seleucus Philopator
2.03	_____ Hercules	c. fortified city taken by Antiochus III
2.04	_____ Berenice	d. (Hebrew name) means *YHWH helps*
2.05	_____ Mishael	e. first wife of Antiochus II
2.06	_____ Laodice	f. daughter of Antiochus III betrothed to young Ptolemy
2.07	_____ Azariah	g. means *Who is like God?*
2.08	_____ Sidon	h. P. Philadelphus' daughter who married Antiochus II
2.09	_____ Ulai	i. artificial canal 900 feet wide
2.010	_____ Belshazzar	j. king who saw God's handwriting on wall

Answer these questions (each answer, 3 points).

2.011   What were the six requirements of young men trained for Nebuchadnezzar's service?

a. _____   d. _____

b. _____   e. _____

c. _____   f. _____

2.012   What were three rewards promised to Daniel by Belshazzar for interpreting the handwriting on the wall?

a. _____

b. _____

c. _____

2.013   At the end of the vision of the four beasts, what did Christ (Son of Man) receive as surrounded by the holy angels and saints of all the ages?

_____

_____

Choose the correct answer (each answer, 2 points).

2.014   *YHWH is gracious* is the meaning of the Hebrew name _____ .

a. Daniel   d. Hananiah

b. Shadrach   e. Meshach

c. Azariah

2.015   Daniel directed Nebuchadnezzar's attention to the God in heaven that reveals _____ .

a. wisdom   d. handwriting

b. lies   e. truth

c. secrets

2.016   The book of Daniel is apocalyptic literature, similar to the book of ____ in the New Testament.

a. Amos   d. Matthew

b. Isaiah   e. Revelation

c. 1 Thessalonians

2.017   The city of _____ was the chief capital of the Persian Empire.

         a. Babylon   d. Susa

         b. Ulai   e. Elam

         c. Media

2.018   The period during which the Jews were persecuted was described by Gabriel as the _____ .

         a. apocalypse   d. fury

         b. wrath   e. indignation

         c. septuagint

Complete these statements (each answer, 3 points).

2.019   Daniel's name means _____ in the Hebrew language.

2.020   As a young boy Daniel may have seen the reforms of idol-smashing King _____ of Judah.

2.021   The book of Daniel was included among the _____ in the Hebrew Bible.

2.022   The word PERES or UPHARSIN means _____ .

2.023   The prophet who wrote of the seventy-year captivity was _____ .

2.024   The book of Daniel was written in both Hebrew and _____ .

2.025   Portions of the book of Daniel is written as _____ literature.

2.026   Daniel's second vision of the ram and the he-goat occurred during the reign of _____ .

2.027   The capital of the Persian Empire was the city of Shushan, or _____ .

2.028   The ruler of the Grecian Empire who defeated the Persians was _____ .

Complete these activities (each answer, 5 points).

2.029   What is the meaning of the 2,300 days of Daniel 8:14?

     _____

     _____

     _____

     _____

2.030   Describe one of the interpretations of the seventy weeks of Daniel 9.

     _____

     _____

     _____

     _____

82 / 103

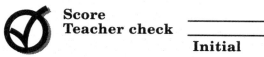

Score

Teacher check _____

                           Initial   **Date**

Before you take the LIFEPAC Test, you may want to do one or more of these self checks.

1. ____ Read the objectives. Determine if you can do them.

2. ____ Restudy the material related to any objectives that you cannot do.

3. ____ Use the SQ3R study procedure to review the material.

4. ____ Review all activities and Self Tests, and LIFEPAC Glossary.

5. ____ Restudy areas of weakness indicated by the last Self Test.

GLOSSARY

apocalyptic. A type of literature containing or pertaining to revelation of historical periods exclusively using symbols and imagery.

atrocities. Acts of enormous wickedness or extreme cruelty.

compatriots. Fellow countrymen.

debauchery. Leading astray morally; seduction from duty or allegiance.

emulation. Desire or ambition to equal or surpass.

evince. To show in a clear manner; to indicate; to manifest; to make evident.

Hellenize. To transform a culture in the likeness of Ancient Greece

ignominious. Shameful, dishonorable, disgraceful; degrading, humiliating.

induce. To lead on to some action, condition, or belief by persuasion or argument; to persuade.

myriad. Ten thousand; a great number.

obliterate. To erase or blot out, leaving no traces; to demolish or destroy all trace.

solicitude. Care or concern.